WOULD YOU RATHER?

ANCIENT EGYPTIANS

First published in Great Britain 2023 by Red Shed, part of Farshore

An imprint of HarperCollins*Publishers*
1 London Bridge Street, London SE1 9GF
www.farshore.co.uk

HarperCollins*Publishers*
Macken House, 39/40 Mayor Street Upper,
Dublin 1, D01 C9W8

Written by Clive Gifford
Illustrated by Tim Wesson

ISBN 978 0 00852178 3

Printed and bound in the UK using 100% Renewable Electricity at CPI Group (UK) Ltd.

001

A CIP catalogue record for this title is available from the British Library.

MIX
Paper | Supporting
responsible forestry
FSC™ C007454

CLIVE GIFFORD • TIM WESSON

WOULD YOU RATHER?

ANCIENT EGYPTIANS

RED SHED

Contents

Introduction

Ancient Egypt was one of the world's first great civilizations, beginning around 3100BCE. It was based around the banks of Africa's longest river, the Nile – with neighbours including the Assyrians, Hittites and Babylonians.

The ancient Egyptians were busy being awesomely clever and creative for more than 2,500 years, building palaces, developing written languages and inventing a huge number of things we take for granted today.

This book is jam-packed with fascinating facts, fun challenges and mind-boggling 'would you rather' questions that will send you on a journey back in time to discover what life was really like in ancient Egypt – to live, work, play, and even rule.

Are you ready?

THE KINGDOMS OF
NORTH AFRICA AND THE MIDDLE EAST

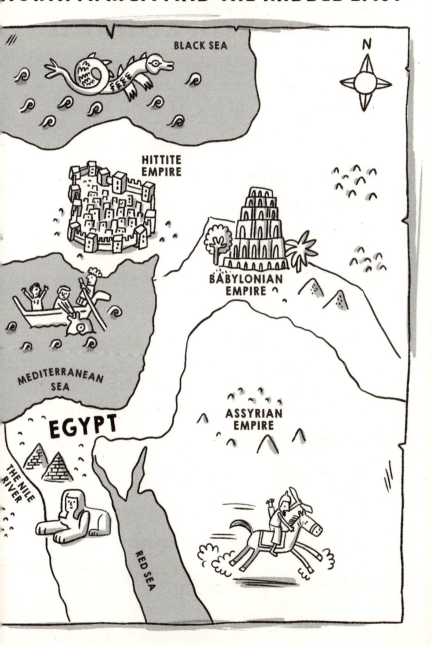

BLACK SEA

N

HITTITE
EMPIRE

BABYLONIAN
EMPIRE

MEDITERRANEAN
SEA

EGYPT

ASSYRIAN
EMPIRE

THE NILE
RIVER

RED SEA

How it all started

So, how did it all begin? Well, *water* start it was! Most of Egypt is very hot, dry and hard to farm. But the area of the region around the Nile river is MUCH easier to grow crops on. The river flooded every year like clockwork, making the soil around it perfect for farming. Early Egyptians quickly realised that this was extremely useful. More crops meant more food, keeping the early ancient Egyptians well fed, full of energy and ready to start building some pyramids. Well, eventually.

As they got nice and comfy (if, at times, a little damp and squelchy) in their riverside homes, the first ancient Egyptians started to get creative. They started to make decorated vases, jewellery and statues, and use symbols to write things down.

The first great rulers of Egypt were the pharaohs, who were thought to be a sort of second-in-command for the gods, in charge of keeping things running smoothly while the gods were off doing more important, godly business. They made laws, built temples, commanded armies and more. All in all, things were hotting up, and the stage was set for a properly EPIC civilization to get up and running.

Read on to get involved . . .

WOULD YOU RATHER

be a rich and powerful pharaoh

OR the sandal bearer who kisses their feet?

IN ANCIENT EGYPT, THE PHARAOHS REALLY RULED THE ROOST AND CALLED THE SHOTS. THERE WERE ABOUT 170 OF THEM DURING THE COURSE OF ANCIENT EGYPTIAN HISTORY, ALL WITH THEIR OWN BELIEFS, INTERESTS AND RULING STYLES ... AND, OF COURSE, HUGE AMOUNTS OF POWER AND WEALTH. BUT WAS IT ALL FUN AND GAMES? WITH GREAT POWER CAME GREAT RESPONSIBILITY ...

Pharaoh

So you've chosen to be a pharaoh, Egypt's big cheese, the head honcho? Ruling Egypt, living in the lap of luxury, with palaces, power, and unimaginable riches? Commanding your lowly subjects to do WHATEVER YOU WANT? Sounds pretty great, doesn't it!

Er . . . actually . . . pharaohs still had a lot of duties to perform. And they weren't all fun.

PHARAOH'S TO-DO LIST

MEET WITH GENERALS TO PLAN ATTACK AGAINST PESKY INVADERS

CHECK ON HEIGHT OF ANNUAL RIVER NILE FLOOD

YAWN!

CHECK TAXES   YAWN!
              (again)

ASK VIZIER (TOP ADVISOR) FOR MONEY FOR
NEW STATUE OF ME!   Much
                           better!

MAKE OFFERING AT TEMPLE TO THE GOD AMUN-RE

OPEN GIFTS FROM VISITING NOBLES

HAVE A BIG LUNCH (OSTRICH, MY FAVOURITE)

GO TO SEE MANY WIVES AND MANY MANY CHILDREN

                enormous
                  v
PLAN DESIGN OF MY TOMB   (and choose riches
                           to fill it with)

Pharaoh
woz ere

15

But a long to-do list might be the least of your worries as ruler. Secret plots to overthrow or kill you would never have been far away. Just ask Ramesses III whose wife plotted his murder . . .

Oh, hang on, you can't – he's dead. Historians also think that some pharaohs who *appeared* to die of natural causes may have actually been poisoned . . .

With all those murder plots, war-mongering and taxes, a pharaoh's life was no picnic. Would those awesome pyramids, the endless adoration and huge stacks of money make up for the pressure and stress of ruling?

Bonus fact

Some pharaohs spent their money on strange things. Tutankhamen owned sandals covered in gold, with soles etched with pictures of foreign leaders Tut didn't like. Every time he took a step, he was crushing Egypt's enemies!

Sandal bearer

You want to kiss a pharaoh's smelly feet?! Unusual choice! But, being the pharaoh's sandal bearer might just be a wise option . . .

For one thing, you'd avoid all the plotting, planning, tax-counting and war-mongering involved with being a pharaoh. Sure, you wouldn't have the fame, power, or massive piles of riches – but you'd avoid the pressure, have a secure job, plenty of food and a roof over your head. Up for it? On to your duties!

SANDAL BEARER'S TO-DO LIST

LOOK AFTER PHARAOH'S SANDALS

ALWAYS CARRY A PAIR OF SANDALS IN CASE HIS
MIGHTINESS REQUIRES A ROYAL CHANGE OF SHOES

BATHE PHARAOH'S FEET

KISS PHARAOH'S FEET BEFORE PUTTING ON HIS SHOES
(NO MATTER IF THEY'VE BEEN WASHED RECENTLY OR NOT!)

Of course, shoes aren't
everything – there was much
more to life as a pharaoh. Turn to
page 66 to meet some of ancient
Egypt's greatest rulers!

EGYPT EXTRAS
Eccentric pharaohs

Pharaohs were not only the rulers of Egypt, they were thought to descend from the gods. They had ultimate authority, godly power, and few people were confident enough to speak up when they were making bad decisions. So, it's not surprising pharaohs sometimes had some bizarre ideas. Here are just a few examples . . .

Fancy a swim?

Queen Tiye was the wife of pharaoh Amenhotep III. He must have been a pretty devoted husband, as he ordered a truly MASSIVE lake to be built for her. It was 1,700m long – that's about the length

of sixteen football pitches laid end to end. Historians are still not 100% sure what it was for, but it definitely would have been big enough for a dip to cool off!

A sticky situation

No one loves being surrounded by flies on a hot day. It's just not pleasant. But King Pepi II took things to another level. He despised flies and other creepy-crawlies, and it's said that he ordered two slaves smeared in honey to stand near him all day so that the flies would ignore him and buzz around *them* instead.

Puntold riches

Obviously, gold and riches are great. However, some pharaohs went much further than others to fill their royal treasure chests. Ramesses III was so keen on gold that he sent his men across the desert . . . IN A BOAT. The idea behind this (rather odd) scheme was to reach the Land of Punt, an ancient kingdom beside the Red Sea, renowned for its incense and gold. To get there, they had to sail down the Red Sea. No biggie, you'd think. Except, on their mission, they had to:

1. Pull their wooden ships off the Nile river and take them to pieces.

2. Haul the parts across 160km of hot, dry desert to the shore of the Red Sea at a harbour called Saww. (They probably lost a few sailors along the way from exhaustion, and the odd ship too.)

3. Rebuild the ships and sail south along the Red Sea to Punt – then do all the above in reverse to get back home. Surprisingly, the expedition does seem to have been a success . . . kerching!

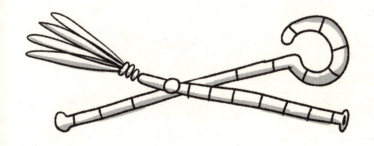

Who gets your prize for quirkiest pharaoh?

WOULD YOU RATHER

be a mummification master

OR a hieroglyph hero?

ARE YOU GOOD WITH YOUR HANDS? OR AN EXPERT WORDSMITH? DO MATHS AND NUMBERS FLOAT YOUR BOAT? WHATEVER YOUR SET OF SKILLS, THERE IS AN ANCIENT EGYPTIAN JOB WAITING FOR YOU ... READ ON TO DISCOVER SOME OF YOUR OPTIONS!

Mummification master

You want to find some bandages and get wrapping? Great! You'll need a strong, steady hand and an even stronger stomach . . .

Being mummified was a complex, expensive process – but pharaohs (and others who could afford it) chose mummification because they believed their bodies would be needed in the afterlife. As a mummy-maker (or embalmer), you need to do a thorough job. Recently-discovered examples, 4,000 or 5,000 years old, are still intact and in good condition.

Let's get to work . . .

Welcome to the
mummy-making academy!

STEP 1

WASH THE BODY
REPEATEDLY IN
WATER AND WINE.

STEP 2

GRAB YOUR LONG, SHARP
KNIVES AND DEADLY HOOKED
INSTRUMENTS AND MAKE
A LONG CUT DOWN THE
LEFT SIDE OF THE BODY.

STEP 3

GET YOUR HANDS IN
AND HAVE A GOOD
ROOT AROUND!

REMOVE THE BRAIN AND THROW IT AWAY. PUT THE LIVER, STOMACH, LUNGS AND INTESTINES CAREFULLY IN SPECIAL CONTAINERS CALLED CANOPIC JARS. THEN TAKE OUT THE HEART, CLEAN IT, AND RETURN IT TO THE DEAD BODY, READY TO BE JUDGED BY THE GODS (SEE PAGE 109).

PACK THE BODY IN NATRON, A SPECIAL KIND OF SALT THAT SUCKS OUT MOISTURE FROM THE BODY.

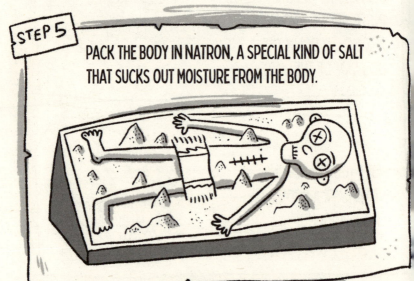

STEP 6

WAIT 40 DAYS OR SO FOR THE BODY TO DRY OUT.

STEP 7

IF PARTS OF THE BODY HAVE GONE A BIT SAGGY, USE SCRAPS OF LINEN, MOSS OR SAWDUST AS STUFFING TO PAD THEM OUT.

STEP 8

GET YOUR BANDAGES! YOU'LL NEED UP TO 1,600M OF LINEN STRIPS - THAT'S ABOUT SEVEN TIMES THE WIDTH OF THE GREAT PYRAMID OF GIZA. SOME OF THE BANDAGES HAD MAGIC CHANTS WRITTEN ON THEM.

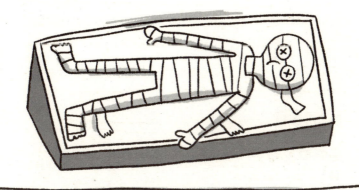

That's a wrap! Would you give mummy-making a go? Or would you rather stick to the land of the living?

Hieroglyph hero

So you've decided that being a scribe would be the *alpha-better* choice? You'd better have a good memory! We learn 26 letters of the English alphabet in school. The ancient Egyptian language didn't have an alphabet. Instead, ancient Egyptians used picture symbols called hieroglyphs. How many symbols do you think scribes had to learn?

a) 28
b) 150
c) over 700

If you guessed **c**, you'd be right! Some symbols were used to describe a single sound, letter or word. Some described a whole idea or object by themselves.

If you wanted to learn hieroglyphs, you'd need to go to scribe school. You'd sit cross-legged on the floor (no chairs and desks) and copy out symbols onto pieces of papyrus or limestone – time and time again, day after day . . .

. . . for 8-12 years. Big commitment.

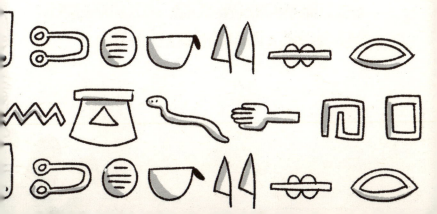

Would it be worth it? Probably.
At a time when next to no one
was literate, being able to read
and write would be like having
a SUPERPOWER. You could have
all kinds of important jobs . . .

COPYING OUT LAWS (TO KEEP THOSE PESKY
CITIZENS IN ORDER).

COLLECTING TAXES (KEEPING YOUR
PHARAOH RICH — IMPORTANT FOR STAYING
ON THEIR GOOD SIDE).

WRITING DOWN YOUR PHARAOH'S THOUGHTS AND
IDEAS (DICTATION). ONE SCRIBE CALLED HOREMHEB
EVEN BECAME A PHARAOH HIMSELF IN 1319BCE!

Of course, there are LOTS more
skills that were useful in ancient
Egypt. Perhaps you'd prefer being
a barber? Go to page 94 to find
out more . . .

Code breaker

People have studied hieroglyphs for centuries trying to figure them all out. We think an equivalent hieroglyphic alphabet that matches ours would read something like this . . .

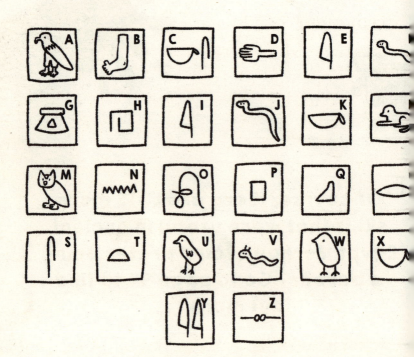

These symbols are all based on real-life objects that would have been known to ancient Egyptians. For example, the N hieroglyph represents water, and Y looks like two reeds. Why not create your own set of hieroglyphs to make coded words?

Whilst you're at it, see if you can decipher this secret message using the code on the opposite page . . .

EGYPT EXTRAS
It all adds up

Are you a maths whizz? Do you know your subtraction from your long division? See how you get on with some ancient Egyptian numbers!

Scribes in ancient Egypt were a smart bunch. Those who were skilled at maths were in great demand to record figures about the pharaoh's kingdom, such as the number of people or sacks of grain – often in order to work out what taxes should be.

To do this, they used a set of special number symbols:

1 – A STICK

10 – A HEEL BONE

100 – A COIL OF ROPE

1,000 – A LOTUS FLOWER

10,000 – A FINGER

100,000 – A FROG (OR TADPOLE)

1,000,000 – THE EGYPTIAN GOD HUH

Huh? Uh-huh! Huh was the god of intelligence and eternity. He was usually shown with his arms held out wide – after all, one million is a big number.

So far, so simple. But, sacks of grain don't always come in nice round numbers like 10 or 10,000. When it came to writing down less straightforward numbers, ancient Egyptians used a very different strategy to today's mathematicians . . .

When we write down the number 276, we only need three digits. The 2 is in the hundreds column, the 7 is in the tens column, and the 6 is in the ones column. Short, simple and effective.

But, in ancient Egypt, things took a little longer. To write down the number 276, scribes would need to draw:

Two coils of rope (200)

Seven heelbones (70)

Six sticks (6)

That's 15 different symbols!

Just imagine writing out 999,999 – you'd need to write out nine frog hieroglyphs, nine finger hieroglyphs and so on. It would end up as a total of 54 symbols for what we write as a six-digit number!

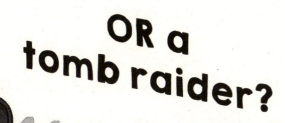

OR a tomb raider?

WELCOME TO THE WORLD OF THE PYRAMIDS! POSSIBLY THE MOST ICONIC, MYSTERIOUS BUILDINGS KNOWN TO HUMANKIND, BUILT TO HOUSE THE BODIES OF DEAD PHARAOHS. THEY WERE FILLED WITH IMMENSE RICHES – AND WERE AN ENDLESS SOURCE OF OPPORTUNITIES!

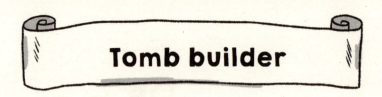

Tomb builder

So you'd prefer a good honest life out on the building site? As a pyramid builder, you'd be playing your part in creating the most MONUMENTAL buildings in history. It would be hard work though.

Great Pyramid of Giza

Height: 146.7m
Width at base: 230.6m

Pyramids needed a lot of stone work, especially the real biggies such as the Great Pyramid of Giza, built for the pharaoh Khufu. It weighs around 6.5 million tonnes, more than a million elephants! You'd have to quarry rocks, chisel them into shape and move them into position, long before cranes, trucks, and other helpful technology.

So, will you be grabbing your toolbag? Or does this simply sound like too much effort . . . ?

Tomb raider

Risky choice! But it could pay off
. . . tomb-robbing was the ultimate
ancient Egyptian get-rich-quick (or die
trying) scheme. Pharaohs and nobles
would fill their tombs with fabulously
valuable possessions, ripe for swiping.
Robbers could either keep the loot or
find a powerful (and corrupt) buyer.

Caught out

If you got caught tomb-raiding, boy, were you in BIG trouble. Egypt had its own court system, which could be harsh. The very least you could expect was a severe beating with a stick or several hundred lashes with a whip. There was also a chance of having your hands or ears cut off with a sharp sword. Owww!

Are you ready for a life of crime? Or will you stick on the straight and narrow? Turn to page 130 to learn even more about Egyptian burials . . .

EGYPT EXTRAS
Revolting remedies

Welcome to the ancient Egyptian doctor's surgery – where YOU are the doctor! Don't hang about, you've got a row of patients waiting. Read through these remedies and get ready to prepare your prescriptions. And make sure you have a strong stomach, as health problems in ancient Egypt were a gruesome business . . .

Cure for baldness

Head out and (VERY carefully) hunt down a hippopotamus, cat, snake and crocodile. Remove some fat from all of them, mix it up in a pan and bring

to the boil. Reduce to a simmer, cool, then slap onto your patient's scalp. Hair raising! (Or maybe not . . .)

Cure for blindness

Take one pig's eye, antimony (a chemical element a bit like lead) and some honey. Grind up the eye, then mix in the antimony. Stir in a little honey to form a paste. Insert paste into your patient's earhole. Recite a spell, and hey presto! Your patient will instantly be cured.

Is it working?*

Cure for loose teeth

You have three options here, lucky you!

Cure 1: Pull out the tooth (hold your nose – judging from scientific analysis of mummies, you can bet your last baby tooth that most Egyptians had rank BAD BREATH).

Cure 2: Tie the loose tooth to a non-wobbly one (like a kind of tooth crutch).

Cure 3: Soak some barley in honey, then put it under the loose tooth to soothe it. Some used a primitive drill to put a hole in a diseased tooth or part of the gum to let pus ooze out. Yuk!

Cure for toothache

Find a dead mouse. Mash up your mouse and put it into your patient's mouth.

Mmmmm. Make sure they don't swallow though, just leave it pressed up against their throbbing tooth. (Look on the bright side, it will give them something else to think about apart from the excruciating pain . . .)

Cure for a head wound

First, examine the wound by sticking your hands right into it. Is it festering and infected? No problem! Go and get some mouldy bread. Place it on the wound and tie it in place with bandages. If you want to be extra sure the cure will work, get your patient to swallow some mouldy bread as well – yuck!

You're all set! Which patient will you be curing first?

WOULD YOU RATHER

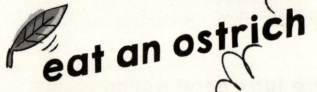

eat an ostrich

OR a raw onion?

DINNER TIME! ALL HARD-WORKING ANCIENT EGYPTIANS NEEDED TO EAT, WHETHER THEY WERE SOLDIERS, BUILDERS OR MIGHTY PHARAOHS. BUT EGYPTIANS FROM DIFFERENT WALKS OF LIFE ENJOYED PRETTY DIFFERENT CUISINES. GET READY TO TUCK IN!

Raw onion

Did you go for the onion? Definitely less hassle to chase down than an ostrich! The menu for poorer Egyptians was very limited, especially for a packed lunch out in the farm fields or on the building site. The most they could hope for was some

Beer

dried bread, beer and one or two raw onions which were eaten whole.

Onions weren't just food for Egyptian farmers and labourers though – they were common food for most ancient Egyptians, and were also eaten by the wealthy. They were thought to have medicinal properties. It's possible ancient Egyptians even used them to represent eternal life. Pharaoh Ramesses IV, who ruled from 1156–1150BCE, was found buried with small onions in his eye sockets, where his eyeballs would have been. They would likely have been placed there by an embalmer (see page 26). They must have been a valued veg!

Ostrich

Did you choose ostrich? Expensive taste! Ostriches were only for the wealthy to eat. These huge birds generally live further south in Africa, but ancient Egyptians kept them on farms for food.

There was plenty of lean meat on an ostrich to feed an ancient Egyptian.

Of course, you'd have to catch one first . . . they run at a top speed of 70km/h, more than twice the speed most Olympic sprinters can run!

Ostriches were also prized for their large feathers, which were used in religious ceremonies, and as fans. Useful in the hot Egyptian sun!

Bonus fact

Ostrich eggs weighed 1.5kg and were eaten in ancient Egypt. Cracking one would give you the equivalent of 24 chicken eggs!

What did you choose? Head to page 117 to learn about more ancient Egyptian delicacies.

EGYPT EXTRAS
Dead good picnic

Making a meal-plan as a living ancient Egyptian was tricky enough – but, they also had to think about what they would eat when they were dead! Pharaohs and wealthy Egyptians would have all their favourite foods carefully wrapped up and stored in their tombs, so they could be sure of a tasty snack on the road to the afterlife.

Honey

Some pharaohs had a sweet tooth! A jar of honey was found in Tutankhamen's tomb – there was still some honey left, thousands of years later!

Meat

In some Egyptian tombs, prime cuts of beef, goat, chicken and other meats were found. The meat was mummified to preserve it, in the same way as humans. Embalmed nuggets, anyone?

Cheese

A cheese over 3,000 years old was once found in an ancient Egyptian tomb. Its owner must have had a *gouda* afterlife!

WOULD YOU RATHER

be an Egyptian soldier

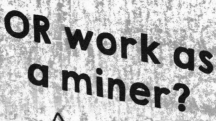

OR work as a miner?

ONCE ANCIENT EGYPTIANS HAD MADE IT THROUGH CHILDHOOD, IT WAS TIME TO START WORK! MOST WEREN'T AS WEALTHY AS THE PHARAOHS, SO SADLY COULDN'T SPEND THEIR TIME LOUNGING AROUND IN HUGE PALACES. BUT THERE WERE A FEW OPTIONS FOR WHAT JOBS THEY COULD DO ...

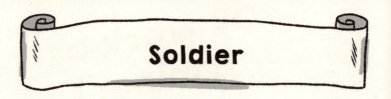

Soldier

Ready to see the world? Good at marching? No problem with hacking the enemy into tiny little pieces? Then, you've made the right choice! A life in the ancient Egyptian army might just be for you.

I'm OK!

There were great career prospects – well, until you were wounded, captured or killed.

If you survived a few battles, you might get promoted to standard bearer where you could be in charge of up to 200 men.

If you built up massive muscly arms and had good eyesight, you might even get plucked from the infantry ranks to become an archer. Some soldiers thought of this as a plum job, partly because you stood over 100m further from the frontline in battles!

Soldiers were often rewarded with slaves, gold or other valuables, depending on how many enemy soldiers they'd killed. Much better than their standard wages – soldiers were usually paid in bread and beer!

Miner

Think you'd prefer to be a miner? You would be responsible for collecting the gold, copper and other precious metals used for jewellery, tools, plates, knives, and more. You'd get to travel out of the hustle and bustle of the city, as most mines were in the desert.

BUT – if you think it's hot on Egypt's desert surface, then wait till you get way below ground. It's roasting! Heaving heavy hammers around would have been hard, uncomfortable work. And to make matters worse, miners would sometimes light fires to weaken the rock, so it could be broken up more easily. If the heat

didn't get you, the toxic smoke might.

Let's be honest, it's not a great option. Most ancient Egyptian miners were slaves who were given no choice.

Will you be heading to war with a sword? Or would you rather work underground with a chisel? If neither of these options appeal, try page 92 for some more job options.

EGYPT EXTRAS
Where's my mummy?

It wasn't only treasure that tomb-raiders across the centuries were after. Sometimes, they made off with the mummies, too! Here are just a few of the strange places stolen mummies could end up . . .

PAINT POTS

In 16th, 17th and 18th century Europe, a type of oil paint called mommia brown became popular – this included a powder made from ground-up mummies! Unsurprisingly, it fell out of favour when artists started to discover where it came from . . .

MEDICINE BOTTLES

Mommia paint wasn't the only use for ground-up mummy powder . . . it's not clear quite when the rumour started, but during the medieval era in Europe and beyond, many believed it to be a cure for all sorts of health problems, from bruising and headaches to stomach ulcers. Yuck!

CROP FIELDS

When tomb-raiders had found lots of mummies but didn't have any takers for medicine or oil paint, they sometimes shipped the mummies to be ground up and used in fertiliser to enrich the soil.

Pharaohs hall of fame

Drum roll, please . . .

**Welcome to the ancient
Egyptian pharaohs
hall of fame!**

Here you will find just a few of the
pharaohs who really left their mark on
the world.

Once you've finished, you can decide
– who gets the top prize for best pharaoh
of them all . . . ?

Tutankhamen
(1341-1323BCE)

When it comes to fame, Tutankhamen
is number one. He is far and away the
best-known pharaoh. He was actually only
a boy when he became pharaoh, and just
19 years old when he died. Most of his big
decisions were probably made by his chief
adviser, a man called Ay.

Tut liked tradition – many of the old
gods had become unpopular under previous
pharaohs, and Tut brought them back
into fashion. But Tut is mostly known
for his EPIC tomb. When a British
archaeologist called Howard Carter and
his team excavated Tutankhamen's tomb

in the 1920s, they found more than 5,000 incredible objects heaped up inside, including multiple chariots, 130 walking sticks, weapons, a 110kg coffin and a death mask made of solid gold!

Bonus fact

Some of the people involved in the discovery of Tut's tomb mysteriously died soon after. It was rumoured that the 'curse of the pharaoh' was behind the deaths . . .

Cleopatra VII
(70/69BCE–30BCE)

Intelligent, beautiful, politically smart –
Cleopatra really did have it all. She was
able to speak many languages, and became
the most famous female pharaoh of ancient
Egypt – and the last. Explore the timeline
to find out more!

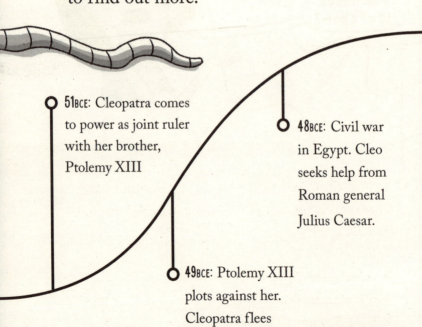

51BCE: Cleopatra comes
to power as joint ruler
with her brother,
Ptolemy XIII

48BCE: Civil war
in Egypt. Cleo
seeks help from
Roman general
Julius Caesar.

49BCE: Ptolemy XIII
plots against her.
Cleopatra flees
Egypt for Syria.

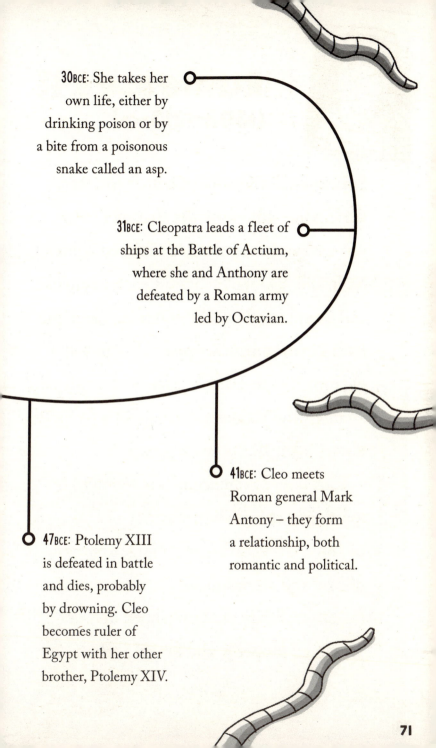

30BCE: She takes her own life, either by drinking poison or by a bite from a poisonous snake called an asp.

31BCE: Cleopatra leads a fleet of ships at the Battle of Actium, where she and Anthony are defeated by a Roman army led by Octavian.

41BCE: Cleo meets Roman general Mark Antony – they form a relationship, both romantic and political.

47BCE: Ptolemy XIII is defeated in battle and dies, probably by drowning. Cleo becomes ruler of Egypt with her other brother, Ptolemy XIV.

Ramesses II
(1303-1213BCE)

Ramesses II was also known as Ramesses the Great – when you get that nickname, you know you've probably achieved a fair bit in life. Ramesses II built more temples and grand royal buildings during his reign than almost any other pharaoh. He had a gigantic temple built at Abu Simbel whilst another, the Ramesseum, contained a huge library with 10,000 papyrus scrolls.

Ramesses II's mummy was found in his tomb near the modern-day city of Luxor in 1881, but wasn't given a huge amount of care and attention. Mummies tend to fall apart if they are unwrapped and not preserved properly, and by 1975, Ramesses was looking the worse for wear. So, he was flown from Egypt to Paris where experts could help repair and restore the mummy. He became the first and, so far, only pharaoh to be issued with a passport. It lists his occupation as: "King (deceased)"!

Hatshepsut
(1507-1458BCE)

Hatshepsut might not be quite as famous as Cleopatra – but she was a pretty kickass female pharaoh. There had only been one or two women who had taken Egypt's top job before her, but this didn't put her off. She ruled for just over 20 years, and made Egypt peaceful and rich. She even wore the fake ceremonial beard that male pharaohs wore. She turned her soldiers into explorers and traders, sending HUGE expeditions to other parts of Africa, including the mysterious land of Punt.

Hatshepsut also ordered a MASSIVE building programme, building or repairing hundreds of statues, pillars and temples.

One of the projects was a temple celebrating her reign, called Djeser-Djeseru. It was GINORMOUS at over 270m wide – that's wider than two football pitches in a row. Much of it still stands today!

So, you've met some of the richest, most powerful pharaohs - but who do YOU think deserves the ultimate pharaoh crown?

WOULD YOU RATHER

spend the day babysitting

OR do all the cooking and cleaning?

ANCIENT EGYPTIAN FAMILY LIFE WAS A BUSY AFFAIR.
UNLESS YOU WERE A PHARAOH LORDING IT IN A PALACE,
YOU'D LIKELY LIVE WITH A LOT OF RELATIVES IN A HOUSE
MADE OF MUD BRICKS. SOUND LIKE FUN? FAMILY LIFE
COULD HAVE ITS DOWNSIDES ...

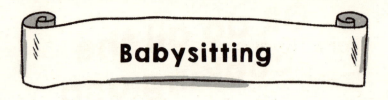

Babysitting

Ahhh . . . nothing like getting home to a bit of peace and quiet, kicking back on the sofa, watching TV . . .

Wait – this is ancient Egypt . . . and you've volunteered for babysitting duty, so roll up your linen sleeves!

Living in an ancient Egyptian home, you would probably be surrounded by relatives. Parents, grandparents, sisters, brothers, aunts, uncles, nieces and nephews would often all live in the same house. Don't panic though – there are lots of things you can do to keep your younger siblings entertained. Here are a couple of ideas to get you started:

Send them outside to play

Out of the way AND getting some exercise – perfect! Ancient Egyptian kids would often play ball games together outside. This helped keep them strong and healthy.

Teach them a lesson

Some ancient Egyptian children would go to school, but usually only if they were from wealthy families (royalty, nobles or government workers). Most children were taught at home and learned the family trade.

Cooking & Cleaning

Think you'd prefer to quietly get on with a spot of housework? In that case, let's write you a list of chores!

1. GRIND WHEAT FOR BREAD AND BEER

Are you *bready*? Wheat was one of the main crops in ancient Egypt, and was the key ingredient for bread and beer. Workers were often given ten pints of beer a day, or more! (Head to page 50 for more on Egyptian food.)

2. FEED YOUR PETS

Many households had a pet – usually

a cat, as they were highly valued in ancient Egypt (see page 120). They would help get rid of pests like scorpions and rats.

3. SEW LINEN CLOTHES

Most clothes were made of linen – a fibre made from flax, a type of plant. Men would wear knee-length kilts (skirts), and women would wear long dresses. Children usually didn't wear clothes at all until they were about six!

What's it to be? Kids or housework? If you need a quick break before you decide, turn the page . . .

EGYPT EXTRAS
Egyptian games

Get ready for family games night! Ancient Egyptians loved a good board game. Here are a few firm favourites . . .

Senet

Each player gets five pieces. The goal is to move all of your pieces around the board and off the other side. Be careful – your opponent can capture your piece if they land on a space you're in.

Mehen

This game is played
on a round board
decorated like a snake.
Each player has four
regular counters and one
lion counter. The aim is to get all of your
counters to the centre of the snake and
back. Your lion has to go last – but it can
'eat' other players' counters!

Hounds and Jackals

This game has two sets of sticks, one set
for each player. One set is shaped like
hounds and the other like jackals. The
sticks fit into holes in the board, and get
raced across the board to find a winner.

WOULD YOU RATHER

fight as a foot soldier

OR as a charioteer?

THE ANCIENT EGYPTIAN ARMY WAS A FORCE TO BE RECKONED WITH. WIELDING THEIR POWERFUL SPEARS, SHARP AXES AND SPEEDY CHARIOTS, EGYPTIAN SOLDIERS WERE EXPERTS AT FIGHTING OFF RAIDERS TO KEEP THE KINGDOM SAFE, AND GOING OUT INVADING.

Foot soldier

So you'd prefer to stay on your own two feet? You'd be kept busy with the Egyptian army's many battles against surrounding kingdoms, like the Hittites, Assyrians, Babylonians (see the map on page 9). It wouldn't be toe-tally awful though – as a foot soldier, you'd be

Are we nearly there yet?

marching here, there and everywhere. You'd see the world, make some friends, get some fresh air and exercise . . .

Actually you'd get a LOT of exercise. You'd often march 20–30km a day, through scorchingly hot, dry desert, carrying all of your kit with you. Did we mention that it would be really, really hot?

Bonus fact

Pharaoh Taharqa is said to have ordered his men to run all day, often covering 30km or more in full kit, whilst he rode alongside in a chariot. All right for some!

Charioteer

Looks like you think being a charioteer sounds like *wheely* nice work! You might just be right. Instead of trudging around all day, you'd speed along with the wind in your hair.

However, it would come at a cost. You'd need to keep a tight grip on your horses' reins, so you'd be racing into battle with no weapon, only some bronze armour to protect you from attack by enemy fighters. You'd also have to share your chariot's cramped standing platform

with a smelly archer. He'd be sweating with all the effort needed to pull back his bow – and your head would be right next to his armpit. Remember, no deodorant in ancient Egypt!

AERODYNAMIC HEADDRESS*

ARROW-PROOF CARRIAGE*

600 HORSE-POWER*

SUPER-FAST WHEELS*

Will it be a military life for you? Or is farming more your thing? If so, head to page 124 to find out more!

* These labels are not historically correct.

EGYPT EXTRAS
Five nasty ways to die in ancient Egypt

Life in ancient Egypt wasn't always fun and games. The average life expectancy was around 35 – if you lived to 40, you'd have done very well. There were also dangers around every corner . . .

Pharaohs would often have their servants sacrificed to help them in their journey to the afterlife. One pharaoh called Djer, who died around 2900BCE, was buried with 318 other people – that's a lot of servant slaying!

A punishment for REALLY serious crimes. Without a body, it was thought to be impossible to enter the afterlife.

Pesky mosquitos would have carried this deadly disease far and wide.

Living by the Nile, you'd need to keep a look out for grumpy hippos. They have a powerful bite that can easily kill a human.

Unpopular pharaohs might be poisoned by political enemies – or even relatives!

EGYPT EXTRAS
Good mourning!

With death being so common, mourning (showing sadness for a dead loved one) was something most people had to do at some point. For some though, it was a career . . .

Amateur mourners

As an amateur mourner, you'd be very, very upset when a friend or family member died. You might take part in rituals as the dead person's body was prepared for the afterlife, but most of the time you would be at home, out of the spotlight.

No, just another professional mourner.

Is that a sandstorm?

Here come the pros

On the other hand, professional mourners were at work ALL the time. Mourners were women who earned money by appearing terribly upset at funerals – they had to cry and howl, rip their clothes, wail and throw dust and dirt over themselves.

Their job lasted from when the person died to when they were buried. This period could have been as long as 70 days – it must have been exhausting!

WOULD YOU RATHER

trim, brush and shave as a barber

OR pray, chant and shave as a priest?

SPENDING TIME IN FRONT OF A MIRROR TO MAKE SURE YOU LOOK YOUR BEST IS DEFINITELY NOTHING NEW. ANCIENT EGYPTIANS LOVED A GOOD PREENING SESSION. HAIR CARE AND SHAVING WERE HIGH ON THE LIST – AND NOT JUST FOR THOSE WHO CUT HAIR FOR A LIVING ...

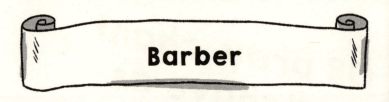

Barber

So you've decided to become a barber? Grab your scissors and comb, and let's have a look at a bit of hair-sterical history!

In early ancient Egypt, beards and thick hair were all the rage. But as ancient Egypt progressed, the facts of living in a hot climate with no soap or shampoo (pee-eew!) made being hairy less and less attractive.

Thinking lice are not so nice, many ancient Egyptian men and some women shaved their faces and heads so their bonces were bald.

So, as a barber, you'd always be in work to keep people's heads smooth and shiny. Your business would have next-to-no start-up costs – just a stool under the shade of a tree, a razor made from metal sheeting (gold was best) and a mirror made of a polished piece of shiny metal.

Bonus fact:

Egyptians invented the first shaving wax, made of beeswax and sugar.

Priest

Ah, you've opted for the religious life instead of getting up close and personal with many, many ancient Egyptian scalps? Nice escape . . . or is it?

As a priest, you'd also have to do plenty of shaving – of yourself. You wouldn't even be paid for it! You'd be expected to shave not just your head, but your ENTIRE body, as

often as once every three days. And that's all in addition to your religious duties such as praying, keeping your shrine and statues nice and clean, more praying, chanting, rituals . . . did we mention praying?

However, being a priest would have its perks. They could be either men or women, and were thought of very highly in society. They were well looked-after, with local people donating food and other goods to them. Priests were the only people allowed to enter all parts of a temple. Some gained power and influence – more than most barbers!

So, will you be *shaving* up for a new razor? Of course, hair care isn't for everyone - head to page 124 to find out what other jobs you could do . . .

EGYPT EXTRAS
Looking for a bargain

Are you ready for your weekly shop? Off to the market with you! But before you go, what do you think would help you get the best deal while haggling at an ancient Egyptian market?

a) Talking really, really fast, or . . .
b) Being very tall and lanky

OK, perhaps both might help. Maybe. But option b would have had some surprising advantages!

You see, for much of the time, ancient Egypt didn't have any precise

measurements (like our centimetres or
inches) that were standard across the
entire empire. The three most common
units of length were all based on body
parts. These measures were:

Digit

The width of your middle finger.

Palm

The side-to-side width of the palm
of your hand.

Cubit

The distance from your elbow up
your lower arm to the tip of your
middle finger.

The cubit was invented around 3000BCE and was a very popular measure. But, all human bodies are a little different – so the actual length of a cubit varied a LOT.

Sending a super-tall brother to collect your shopping would get you more of anything sold for a fixed price per cubit than if you went yourself, simply because his cubit was a lot longer than yours. It was one reason why especially tall slaves were in great demand.

Eventually, ancient Egyptians decided that more precise measures would be fairer, and introduced standardized royal cubits made out of black granite, a type of rock. Market officials from all over Egypt would make their own wooden measuring sticks matching the royal cubit, check traders' measurements, and fine anyone using a too-long or too-short measure. Spoilsports!

Gods hall of fame

Welcome back to the ancient Egyptian hall of fame – this time, for the gods! There were THOUSANDS of gods in ancient Egypt, who were associated with different things, such as the moon, music or the underworld.

Here are just a few of the many Egyptian gods. Once you've read all about these mysterious deities, it's over to you – who is *your* favourite?

Isis & Osiris

This husband-and-wife duo were a truly iconic pair, and two of the most important and popular gods in Egyptian history.

According to mythology, Osiris was murdered by his brother, Set, who cut him up into tiny pieces and scattered him all over Egypt. Rude.

Thankfully, Isis saved the day. With the help of a few other gods,

she gathered up all the pieces and put him back together. Osiris was then embalmed (becoming the very first mummy!) and headed down to the underworld where he took his place as King of the Dead. Fancy job!

Meanwhile in the myth, Isis and Set were still hanging around in the land of the living, and Isis was pregnant with Osiris' baby. Isis soon gave birth to little Horus, and kept herself busy protecting him from crocodiles and scorpions – and hiding from Set to avoid any more body chopping. Eventually, when Horus was old enough, he successfully battled Set, became ruler of Egypt and took his place as one of the most worshipped gods of all. Winner!

Anubis

This god was a dark and mysterious guy. He had the head of a jackal (a kind of Egyptian wild dog) and was the god of death, mummies and the afterlife – so it's not completely surprising that he spent most of his time hanging around dead people (and their guts).

He probably would have made ancient Egyptians a wee bit nervous as they lay on their deathbeds. This was because Anubis was involved with the Weighing of the Heart – one of the first, scariest and most important events in an Egyptian's journey to the afterlife . . .

The Weighing of the Heart

During mummification, the heart was left in the body (see page 28 for more). This was so that Anubis could give it a careful weighing, to work out if its owner was worthy of entering the underworld.

The heart would go on one side of Anubis' scales. On the other side would be a feather (representing truth). If your heart was heavier than the feather, you could kiss goodbye to any chance of a cosy afterlife. It would be thrown straight to Ammut, a monstrous goddess with a crocodile's head, who would promptly gobble it up!

Hathor

Hathor was the goddess of the sky, fertility and love, and was a go-to god for ancient Egyptian women (though she did have male followers).

She was also associated with music . . . and wild parties! Hathor's temples got LOUD during the many religious festivals of the ancient Egyptian calendar. Party-goers – *ahem* – *worshippers* would often play instruments

like the harp and the sistrum (a percussion instrument similar to a rattle) in her temples.

(She was also often shown as a cow –
she must have had some great dance
*mooo*ves . . .)

Hathor was also important for ancient
Egyptians travelling to faraway lands.
Being the goddess of the sky, she
was also goddess of stars. These were
important tools for navigation at sea,
as they were fixed points that sailors
could use to work out which direction
they were heading in. Sailors would
look to Hathor for protection on their
long voyages.

Ra

He might have a short name, but Ra was one of the BIGGEST gods around in ancient Egypt. He had the head of a sleek, speedy falcon, and was the god of the sun and creation. Ra also had a big part to play in the cycle of day and night . . .

A day in the life of Ra

Ra lit up the world by sailing across the sky in a huge sun-boat. Epic, right?

Every morning, Ra would head out into the clouds, no doubt enjoying the adoration of all the happy Egyptians down below.

BUT – lying in wait for him was a HUGE scary serpent god called Apep. Every evening, Ra would have to leave his sun-boat behind and get into his nighttime boat, ready to do battle with Apep in the underworld.

Of course, being the strong, powerful, god-boss that he was, he'd win every night. With Apep vanquished, Ra would get back into his sun-boat, ready to do the whole thing again . . . and again . . .

Of course, there were MANY more gods in ancient Egypt - but which god gets your vote?

WOULD YOU RATHER

monkey around as a baboon

OR pad about as a claw-some cat?

ANIMALS OFTEN HELD A SPECIAL POSITION IN
ANCIENT EGYPTIAN HEARTS, FOR BOTH PHARAOHS
AND LOWER-CLASS WORKERS. MANY WERE
CONNECTED WITH GODS, SUCH AS THE JACKAL (SEE
PAGE 108). TURN THE PAGE TO READ MORE ABOUT
ANIMALS IN THE ANCIENT EGYPTIAN WORLD …

Pet pandemonium

Before you get started, you might need a bit more info about animals in the ancient world. To be honest, many ancient societies thought of animals as only good for two things – food and manual labour.

HEDGEHOG

GOOSE

OX

HIPPO

Ancient Egyptians, though, were a little different. They kept a range of animals as pets. In fact, only one of the animals pictured below was NOT kept as a pet. Can you guess which?

It's the hedgehog! They were found in some ancient Egyptian households, but only as food – mice also counted as a tasty Egyptian snack. So, now you've got the facts, back to the baboons and cats!

BABOON

CROCODILE

HOPE YOU DIDN'T ANSWER, "CROCODILES" OR "HIPPOS"... THESE WERE BOTH KEPT BY WEALTHIER PEOPLE AS A STATUS SYMBOL!

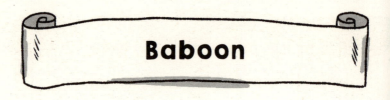

Baboon

Do you think you're a monkey-business expert? Baboons were kept as pets by some wealthier ancient Egyptian households. Agile, smart and strong-willed, baboons were appealing as they were linked to the Egyptian god of wisdom and scribes, called Thoth.

They were also liked because they raise their heads and bark at the sun in the morning, like they were greeting the rising sun. As big sun-worshipping people, the ancient Egyptians were seriously impressed.

Some Egyptian baboon-owners tried to train their pets to climb tall date and fig

trees and do the fruit-picking for them.
Paintings of this have been found in
temples and tombs. However, it might
have been that the baboons ate more
of the fruit than they actually brought
down for their owners . . .

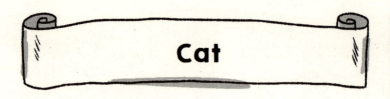

Cat

Are you *feline* the life of a cat? Great choice! Cats lived a life of LUXURY in Egypt, especially in wealthy families, with collars studded with precious jewels, servants to attend their every need and food fit for a pharaoh. They were thought to have magical powers and bring good luck. Thousands of cats were even mummified and buried in their owners' tombs!

Bonus fact:

When a pet cat died, its owners would often display their grief by shaving their eyebrows off!

A visitor to Egypt in the fifth century BCE called Herodotus was astonished at how close many Egyptians were to their cats. He wrote that when an Egyptian's home caught fire, the owners would save their cat before their possessions and even, sometimes, their children.

So, will you be monkeying around as a baboon? Or enjoying a well-earned cat-nap? For more on Egypt's majestic moggies, turn the page . . .

EGYPT EXTRAS
Cat battle!

Most of the time, cats were happily curled up in their comfy Egyptian mud houses. But, they were once used on the battlefield in a cruel trick against the Egyptians by an enemy army . . .

THE BATTLE OF PELUSIUM 525BCE

PHARAOH PSAMETIK III CAMBYSES II OF PERSIA

WINNER: THE PERSIANS

Cambyses II was the king of Persia, an empire in the area of modern-day

Iran, north-east of Egypt. He was keen to expand his territory, and knowing the Egyptians' devotion to cats, clever Cambyses had his men round up lots of cats and then drive them towards the Egyptian army. He also ordered his soldiers to paint cats on their shields.

As the Persians – and the cats – advanced, the Egyptians retreated, as they were terrified of harming their furry friends. The Egyptians eventually surrendered and the Persians captured the city of Pelusium. It's said that Cambyses gloated and threw cats at the defeated Egyptians as he rode through the city he'd captured.

What a cat-astrophe!

WOULD YOU RATHER

be a farmer

OR a fisher?

THE NILE RIVER, THE LONGEST RIVER IN THE WORLD, RAN THROUGH ANCIENT EGYPT AND WAS IMPORTANT FOR TRANSPORT, PRODUCING FOOD, AND MORE. BUT WHILE THE RIVER WAS IN ALL EGYPTIANS' LIVES, SOME RELIED ON IT MORE HEAVILY THAN OTHERS TO MAKE A LIVING ...

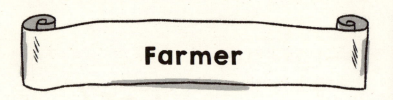

Farmer

So you've decided to grab a plough and take to the fields? Hope you don't mind getting your feet wet – the Nile river would be a big part of your life . . .

ANCIENT EGYPT: THREE SEASONS

MUD TIME

GRUB TIME

FLOOD TIME

Ancient Egyptian farmers needed the Nile to keep their wheat, barley, beans and other crops well-watered during the many months of the year when it was hot and dry. Smart farmers stored water in reservoirs made of mud bricks, some dug channels to carry water to their fields.

Farmers who lived closest to the river had less distance to go for water. This was a big perk, but it also came with a BIG risk. Every year (usually in June), the Nile flooded its banks, submerging fields. Some farmers' entire homes, made of mud bricks, would be washed away.

On the bright side, if you survived the flood, you'd be left with lovely moist fields when the flood drew back – much easier to sow and grow new crops!

Fisher

Think you'd rather take to the water than water the fields? Prefer boats to oats? Grab your net and jump on board!

As a Nile fisher, you'd most likely have a small boat made of river reeds tightly woven together, and a net made of tied-together linen cords. When you weren't on the water, you'd be busy with repairs. Hope you're good with knots . . .

Out on the river, there'd be plenty of fish to catch, including catfish, mullet and eels. You'd have to watch out for hippos though, who like nothing more than tipping boats over, and are famously unfriendly to humans.

Any other spare time would be spent gutting and cleaning your catch, ready for trading . . . oh, and trying to get rid of that tell-tale fishy smell that would be hanging around you at all times!

What's it to be – fields or fish? Sowing or sailing? For more ancient Egyptian jobs, go to page 58!

WOULD YOU RATHER

be buried in a huge pyramid

OR in a tomb at the Valley of the Kings?

PHARAOHS IN ANCIENT EGYPT WOULD SPEND A FAIR BIT OF TIME PREPARING FOR THEIR OWN DEATH. A BIG TOMB AND PLENTY OF FOOD AND TREASURE TO GO IN IT WERE A MUST, AS THE PHARAOH WOULD NEED TO BE WELL-PREPARED FOR THE AFTERLIFE. BUT, TYPES OF TOMBS DID CHANGE A BIT OVER THE YEARS ...

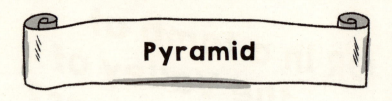

Pyramid

There are no two ways about it – pyramids are cool. People would certainly sit up and take notice if you chose one of these giant tombs for your final resting place. Need some inspiration before you start building? Let's take a closer look . . .

Step right up!

First, you'd need to decide how your pyramid looks on the outside. The Great Pyramids of Giza have flat sides, but some earlier pyramids had sides made up of huge steps. These step pyramids were a bit simpler to design and build.

Feeling sneaky?

Obviously, with a huge pyramid, everyone will know where you're buried. You might want to consider some sneaky fake passages and chambers to trick any would-be thieves!

Interior decor

Plain old stone can get a bit boring – some wall paintings describing your life and your journey to the underworld might help liven the place up.

Valley of the Kings

If you'd like your resting place to be comfortable, but a little less flashy, the Valley of the Kings is an excellent choice. This quiet valley in the desert opposite the city of Thebes was filled with tombs built deep into the rock, all designed to keep the pharaohs inside them well-hidden and ready for their journey to the afterlife.

Sadly, like the pyramids, most of these tombs were raided over time. Most of the tombs had several rooms full of swag – too much for some robbers to resist.

One tomb that DID escape being ransacked was King Tutankhamen's. This was mainly because the entrance was covered up with rubble from other tombs. Head to page 68 for more . . .

Which would you choose? Show-off pyramid or hidden tomb?

How it all ended

In the last thousand years or so of ancient Egypt, there were many wars and invasions. Assyrians, then Persians took control of the area, until they were booted out in 332BCE by the wealthy and ambitious leader of the Macedonian army, Alexander the Great. His followers formed the Ptolemaic Kingdom – the last phase of ancient Egypt.

After a good few Ptolemaic pharaohs (funnily enough, all named Ptolemy) had been and gone, Cleopatra VII became pharaoh (head back to page 70 for more on her reign). She was clever and powerful, but eventually, she was defeated by a different great civilization: ancient Rome. Egypt was taken over by Roman Emperor Octavian (who later called himself Augustus) and became part of the Roman Empire. As Octavian was far too busy to rule Egypt himself, he appointed a special Roman governor to keep things running smoothly.

And that was the end of that – Egypt had started a whole new phase of its history, with plenty more conquests, quirky rulers, gods, customs and traditions to come. But ancient Egypt had firmly left its mark, in art, culture, science, language and more – not to mention the huge pyramids and temples that are still standing today!

Glossary

Afterlife – the life ancient Egyptians believed they would live after they died, if they were given the proper burial rituals.

Archer – a soldier who fought with a bow and arrows.

Assyrians – people of Assyria, an ancient civilization north-east of Egypt.

Babylonians – people of Babylon, an ancient civilization in the area of modern-day Iraq.

Chariot – a wheeled cart, often used in battles.

Embalming – the process of preserving a dead body.

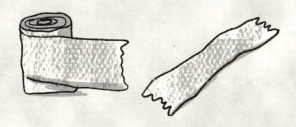

Hieroglyphs – picture-like symbols that made up the ancient Egyptian written language.

Hittites – an ancient people from the area of modern-day Turkey.

Mummy – an embalmed body of an ancient Egyptian, wrapped in bandages and preserved.

Papyrus – a type of paper used in ancient Egypt, made from a type of plant.

Persians – an ancient people from the area of modern-day Iran.

Pharaoh – an ancient Egyptian ruler, believed to have a connection with the gods.

Pyramid – a huge three or four-sided structure, built as a tomb for a pharaoh.

Romans – an ancient people who were part of a huge civilization that emerged from the area of modern-day Italy.

Scribe – an ancient Egyptian whose job was writing things down.

Underworld – a place to which ancient Egyptians believed they would journey in the afterlife.

Vizier – a high-ranking official who often worked as an advisor to an ancient Egyptian pharaoh.

About the author

Clive Gifford is an old relic but not quite as old as the pyramids. He has travelled to more than 60 countries including Egypt which he has visited five times, exploring the Temple of Karnak and descending into the tombs of rulers in the Valley of the Kings. Clive has written more than 200 books for children and adults, and has won the Royal Society, SLA and Blue Peter book awards. He lives in Manchester, UK.

About the illustrator

As a young boy, Tim Wesson was
constantly doodling, finding any excuse
to put pen to paper. Since turning his
much loved pastime into his profession,
Tim has achieved great success in the
world of children's publishing, having
illustrated and authored books across a
variety of formats. He takes great delight
in turning the world on its head and
inviting children to go on the
adventure with him.

Explore the rest of the series for more fascinating facts and hilarious WOULD YOU RATHER questions!

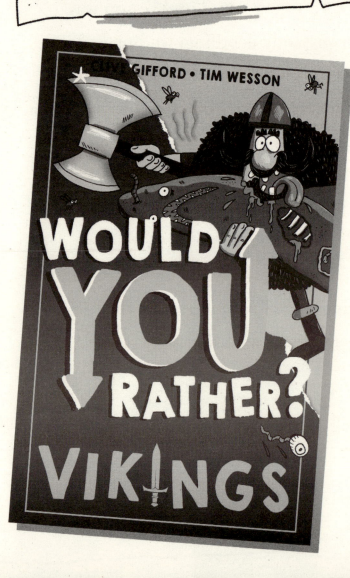

to have actually met you. You're my biggest inspiration.' She looked up at the old moth, happy tears filling her eyes. 'I've always wanted to follow in your flutterings. Thank you for never giving up on moon magic.'

Lunora smiled. 'Thank YOU, Marnie Midnight, for never giving up on me.'